COMMON SIGHTS

CONRAD ATKINSON

Common Sights

THE WORDSWORTH TRUST

Acknowledgments

Conrad Atkinson shows courtesy of Ronald Feldman Fine Art, New York.

With thanks to Margaret Harrison and Sophy Atkinson for their research and advice; to Kathy Helen, my studio assistant; to Robert Woof, Stephen Hebron, Alex Black, Philip Northcott and all at the Wordsworth Trust for their patience in the face of my unreasonable demands; thanks too to Steve Dixon for his technical advice in developing the ceramics; and to Cathy Paulk in Woodlands, California for her work on Wordsworth's suit. Finally, a special thanks to Will Carr for his attention to detail and for all his help in practical matters.

Conrad Atkinson, November 2003

The contemporary arts programmes at the Wordsworth Trust are generously supported by Arts Council England, North West; the Northern Rock Foundation; the National Lottery through Arts Council England; the Esmée Fairbairn Foundation; the Garfield Weston Foundation; the Paul Hamlyn Foundation; Cumbria County Council; South Lakeland District Council and the Granada Foundation.

ARTS COUNCIL ENGLAND

northern rock foundation

Published in 2004 by the Wordsworth Trust, Dove Cottage, Grasmere

Designed by Stephen Hebron

Printed by Titus Wilson, Kendal

ISBN 1 870787 89 7

Contents

Conrad Atkinson and William Wordsworth

ROBERT WOOF

Opposite: William Wordsworth by Henry Edridge, 1805

CONRAD ATKINSON and Wordsworth's Grasmere may not seem a natural alliance, but both men breathed the West Cumbrian air. Wordsworth, born in Cockermouth 1770, became a radical and supported the French Revolution, especially during his time in Blois 1791–1792, so he was the only great European writer to be in the midst of that early flowering of new ideas and ideals that preceded the reign of terror of 1793. Conrad Atkinson grew up in the mining village of Cleator Moor, a community marked by forceful radicalism in its politics; you could remember Fletcher Christian, the first mate on *HMS Bounty*, who in 1789 had mutinied against the strict order that Captain Bligh attempted to impose. Then there is John Dalton, another original, born near Cockermouth, who precisely 200 years ago reordered chemistry by publishing the Periodic Table in 1803, and ensured the science on which an industrial future might be based. By the late 1970s, Conrad Atkinson was noting with admiration some words of Wordsworth, written in 1833, that show that although Wordsworth was 'known to the world as a poet', he had 'given twelve hours of thought to the conditions and prospects of society for one to poetry'. That meditation on 'the conditions and prospects of society' underpins Conrad Atkinson's art as it did the profound realism, the matter-of-fact basis of the poetry of Wordsworth.

There are other nuances to link Conrad Atkinson with Wordsworth: throughout Conrad Atkinson's endeavours as a visual artist there has, to some extent, been a need to draw words, text, indeed literature itself, into his art. Beyond Wordsworth, to whom we shall return, or beyond Shelley whose pamphleteering poem *Queen Mab*, with its agenda of feminism, vegetarianism and the inevitability of progress Conrad admires, one of Conrad Atkinson's favourite authors is Emily Brontë. If you look at a page of Emily Brontë's handwriting – squat, squarish letters, miniscule in height – at first glance you feel excluded. But Charlotte describes herself coming upon these indeed 'secret' writings of her sister and feeling overwhelmingly that they should be published. Conrad Atkinson's texts – his works of art – should also be 'read' and appreciated – but, of course, from his audience, energy is required. Thus, Wordsworth's phrase that 'every common sight' no longer seemed 'Apparell'd in celestial light' will not allow a lachrymose reading that this is a personal mourning of loss; rather, he sees it as a general state of alienation which he can see connected in time and place and people. Conrad's wish is to avoid that 'English whimsy' that is found in the great English landscape tradition: his fear is that unless the artist takes proper account of 'the conditions and prospects of society', he will not have that significant and integrated structure of the world of the twenty-first century.

SUN
TUMULTUOUS HARMONY AND FIERCE
SEE PAGE 3 IRAQ BLAIR AND WORDSWORTH
SUN
LYRICAL BALLADS
BECKHAM + WORDSWORTH
WORDSWORTH EDITION
WITH THOUGHTS THAT ARE FED BY THE SUN, AND HOPES THAT ARE WELCOME EVERYONE, HAPPY AM I
NEXT WEEK COLERIDGE DRUG SENSATION
DAILY Mirror
BLISS
AND THESE WE ADORE
SIGHT
DREST FOR SHOW
ink opium like
diet laudanum
Wordsworthburger

Opposite: Conrad Atkinson, working drawing for 'Common Sights', 2003.

It's an odd axiom, but, arguably, every artist of originality, even such an established one as Conrad Atkinson, must provide out of himself, and so create within us, the energy required to understand him. Wordsworth said that every artist, insofar as he is great and original, must teach the art by which he is to be understood. The issue goes beyond the intricacies of the written word: for Wordsworth, poetry was a way of thinking through images, whether working through narrative, high style or low style, with intricate rhyming, the musical phrase, rhythmic patterning. Indeed, to go to another of Atkinson's heroes, Coleridge, we have the suggestion that there was truly 'a danger' in 'thinking without images'. The working of the imagination, in any art form, involves process and changes which have their own logic, and even subtly act beyond the control of the artist's rational mind. Everyone knows of novelists who report that their plots work out in completely unplanned directions. The element of inventiveness and surprise in Conrad Atkinson's work leads to new images, or new voices: somehow we need new songs, even rough voices, to speak freshly to our ear.

Conrad Atkinson is an artist who shares with Wordsworth that sense that this is 'the world / Of all of us, the place in which, in the end, / We find our happiness, or not at all' (*The Prelude* 1805, x, 725–7). Atkinson and Wordsworth share something of the tradition of the novelist: one foot at least is on the ground, which is the 'world of all of us'; and the other part of their art is concerned with what could be and even what should be. Such artists are willing to be admonitory: for Atkinson, attention must be paid to Northern Ireland, to land-mines all over the world; in these artists' zest for life, they are willing to be minatory – not so much the head above the parapet, but the finger; and, if necessary, two fingers. When Wordsworth puts on Juvenalian tones, dignified but hugely disturbed by his own world, we get great sonnets: 'Milton! thou should'st be living at this hour: / England hath need of thee: she is a fen / Of stagnant waters'. Wordsworth wouldn't stop there, and nor would Conrad Atkinson. He would have you look at the past and its achievements, and make you aware of how fragile our present is: a landmine in Iraq, or Mozambique, or Cleator Moor, or at Grasmere – among the paintings, books, watercolours, and original manuscripts of the Romantics – is equally offensive and threatening. And yet, this is not just preaching. The moral intention of an artist does not govern the outcome of his imaginative journey.

I once had the privilege of being taught by Marshall McLuhan, the man who invented such phrases as 'the global village' and 'the medium is the message'; the man who recognised that a car can be like a suit of clothes, and that you can sell it by making it an 'object of desire', the mechanical bride. His analysis sought not to praise the new media, but rather to fear them and to insist that we must devise a language with which we could confront them. He was acute at looking at the newspaper page and pointing out that its fragments based on global happenings were an image of our everyday society: one culture juxtaposed to another: India versus Pakistan; Sierra Leone against itself; Kosovo; Afghanistan; Iraq to be rebuilt; crime in cricket and drugs in sport; BNFL, Foot and Mouth Disease within the economy of West Cumbria; tribalism and racism in both the Congo and metropolitan London. We can, each of us, look through the newspaper and declare, after a couple of hours, 'there is nothing in it'. Conrad Atkinson is likely to take the emptiness of our newspaper and shift its fragments into inconvenient significance and meanings.

One could say that art makes nothing happen; one could also say that newspapers make nothing happen. To Conrad Atkinson, that 'nothing' is not acceptable. Amongst all the visual design, Conrad Atkinson has a peculiar skill with words which he might drop in as a slogan or as graffiti; we are made to recognise that out of these scraps of irritated reaction to this world that is the world of all of us, out of these fragments of moral tetchiness, Atkinson suggests that boredom will not be enough: if we are to find our happiness, it will be touched by consciousness and perhaps conscience.

Conrad Atkinson: a New Beginning

RICHARD CORK

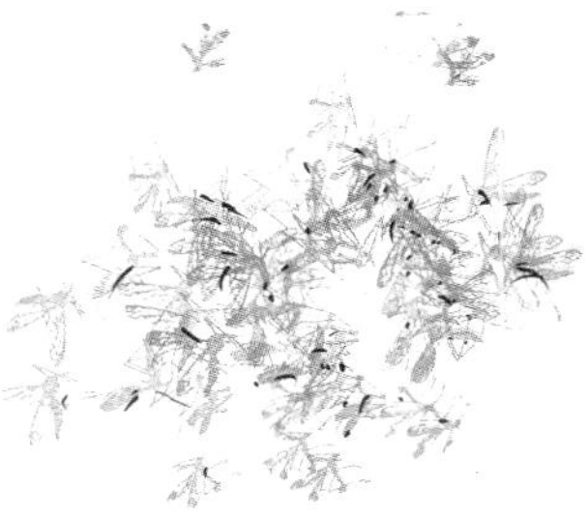

He intended it as a terminal gesture, concluding his involvement with art once and for all. But when the ICA invited Conrad Atkinson to show at its resplendent metropolitan premises overlooking The Mall, his first London exhibition ended up turning into a new beginning.

The year was 1972, and he had spent most of the previous decade training and then practising as an artist in the modernist tradition. After studying at his local College of Art in Carlisle and then Liverpool, he took his painting degree at the Royal Academy Schools in London. Over that six-year period, Atkinson moved from the austere figurative idiom of his resolute nineteen year-old self-portrait to large abstract canvases. He may have called some of them the Hiroshima series, in the hope that his form of abstraction could somehow grapple with the shaping political events of the twentieth century. But he never felt at ease with the alien world of West End dealers and galleries. 'I felt like a working-class astronaut in middle-class space', Atkinson recalled later, and only a couple of years after graduating he virtually abandoned his commitment to painting.

Having gone to Carlisle College imagining that art was a central activity, he came to the conclusion in the late 1960s that it had become hopelessly marginalised. The work he was encouraged to produce, during his student years, bore no relation to the world he grew up in during and immediately after the Second World War. His childhood had been spent in Cleator Moor, a depressed West Cumbrian area where the closure of coal-mines was creating widespread unemployment. Atkinson's grandfather, who exerted a powerful influence on the boy, had played an active and respected role in the community. As the miners' agent and union man in West Cumberland, he was an outspoken fighter for workers' rights. Most of the people on the housing estate where Atkinson's family lived were Irish Catholics, descended from immigrants who had crossed the sea to find work as miners in the Victorian era.

Towards the end of the Second World War, when Atkinson was around five years old, he helped his grandfather finish a painting of a silver hammer and sickle on a red sheet. They displayed it outside the window of their council house at the heart of the estate, possibly to celebrate a notable Russian victory against Hitler. Atkinson never forgot this formative experience, which involved using a paintbrush to produce an image hung, for everyone to see and understand, in the middle of a tight-knit community. Although he eventually realised that life in West Cumberland was claustrophobic, the values upheld by his family encouraged him to believe in the importance of culture and education. Old Labour supporters knew that colleges could provide the key to a better existence, and Atkinson's parents were impressed when he won a prize for designing a book jacket. They

Opposite: Conrad Atkinson, 'Miners Monument', 1 of 3 peices, 1988.

approved of his decision to study art in Carlisle, and his grandfather undoubtedly felt that 'the finer things of life' could enhance everyone's surroundings. In this respect, William Morris's influence still lingered in socialist circles, but it was very far removed from the priorities of an art-school generation for whom Jackson Pollock and the New York avant-garde were supreme. The more Atkinson studied at his successive colleges, the more estranged he felt from the beliefs that had governed his boyhood.

In order to recover his lost sense of an engagement with contemporary issues, Atkinson turned away from painting in 1967 and began producing posters. They were focused, with polemical intent, on political causes of the day, most dramatically the tragic spate of assassinations that destroyed Martin Luther King, Bobby Kennedy and Malcolm X. But poster-making did not solve the main problem confronting Atkinson at that turbulent time, when the entire activity called 'art' was being challenged and redefined in so many different ways by the emergent generation. He felt increasingly dissatisfied with the level of debate, which often remained at a philosophical level and avoided acknowledging the importance of subject-matter.

That is why Atkinson responded so defiantly to the ICA's invitation. He was only prepared to mount a show there if it took the form of an attack on art. Conceived as a disenchanted farewell rather than an auspicious debut, the exhibition was pitched at the rawest possible level. And Atkinson deliberately turned back to his roots, telling the ICA that there was only one thing he intended to deal with: the current strike in his home town.

A year before, Brannan Thermometers Factory on Cleator Moor had become the arena for a major dispute. The management gave certain members of the work-force a privileged status, and the rest of the factory reacted with indignation. In June 1971 they withdrew their labour, announcing that the preferential treatment was at once arbitrary and unjustified. Since the management refused to respond, the dispute focused on the workers' right to be consulted and have a say in their own conditions. Outside help was brought in to keep the factory running, but eighty union members continued to picket Brannan's day and night. Since Atkinson had gone to school with many of the strikers, he felt passionately about their predicament and wanted to help them bring about significant change. So he set to work, amassing a formidable amount of carefully researched evidence from the battleground itself.

All this material was used in the ICA exhibition. Tersely entitled *Strike*, it included letters, written statements, photographs and interviews constantly transmitted on three video monitors. The show as a whole refused to rely on the impact of a documentary programme, where everything is summarised and punched across with an emphasis on dramatic effect. Instead, Atkinson provided the viewer with a mass of data which could only be absorbed fully after prolonged, detailed scrutiny. His own loyalties could be discerned, above all in the emotive contrast between photographs of the factory owners' resplendent houses and the stark hardship so evident in the workers' home surroundings. *Strike* ended up unequivocally condemning the management, but it adopted the tone of an enquiry rather than a polemic.

Conrad Atkinson, detail from 'For West Cumbria, for Wordsworth', 1981; striking workers in Cleator Moor.

The gallery was even transformed into an arena for a well-attended meeting of strikers and local MPs. Considerable publicity was generated, drawing national attention to a dispute that had failed, initially, to attract the press coverage it deserved. Women's groups joined in the discussions, reflecting their awareness that the strike had largely been organised by a dedicated women's work-force. Atkinson made prints for sale at the exhibition, to help raise money for the strike fund. And as a result of all these efforts, Brannan's London factory was unionised. It was an remarkable victory, proving that artists can indeed have direct political effect if their focus is defined with sufficient clarity and conviction.

Judged as a work of art, though, *Strike* was considered less successful. Writing in the *Evening Standard*, I agreed that 'the medium of an art exhibition does provide a marvellously free forum for the promotion of such a committed viewpoint.' But I concluded that, compared with a television programme on the same subject, 'this gallery-full of data seems undeniably hamfisted.' The final word stung Atkinson into writing a pugnacious letter to the *Evening Standard*. We subsequently exchanged correspondence and met for the first time. The following year, he contributed a work called *Wage Differential* to my Critic's Choice exhibition in London. More tightly organised and refined than *Strike* had been, it prophesied the direction Atkinson would take in his 1974 show at the ICA.

Although *Work, Wages and Prices* did not target a solitary example of industrial conflict, it shared *Strike's* belief in taking social injustice as its theme. To this extent, Atkinson still aimed at changing the consciousness of exhibition visitors by inviting them to think in a harder, more concentrated way about his chosen subject. On another level, however, *Work, Wages and Prices* was directed at an art audience rather than the world of strikers, unions and bosses that he had addressed in his previous ICA show. In *Strike*, one wall was devoted to worker/management while the other concentrated on meetings and fundraising. In *Work, Wages and Prices*, by contrast, the principal argument was put forward in a sequence of printed cards running relentlessly round the room's four walls.

The very first card announced the principal thrust of the exhibition with startling clarity: 'Wealth is considerably more unequally distributed in Britain than in the United States despite all its millionaires and billionaires.' Anyone who doubted the accuracy of that statement was subjected, in the remaining cards, to a barrage of examples. The salaries of the wealthiest were spelled out, and contrasted with the abject take-home pay of the poorest. The burgeoning price of property in the most expensive areas of London was set against the alarming number of homeless families in the same metropolis. And the capricious, self-indulgent eating habits of the rich were placed in the gruesome context of an old woman who had died on Christmas Eve, after desperately struggling to keep alive by devouring cardboard.

While visitors followed the devastating analysis spelled out in the cards, they became aware of the pay-slips running along the walls above. The figures printed there disclosed just how wretched the income of a farm worker, a railway maintenance man or a student nurse really was. Then, on a visual level, the conditions endured by the work-force in a factory was revealed in a strip of contact prints. And finally, at the very top, Atkinson displayed a ticker-tape reel from the Stock Exchange registering the incessant changes in the price of shares.

There seemed to be no escape from the evidence marshalled there, like exhibits in a particularly damning court-room prosecution. Elsewhere in the room a trio of screens transmitted images from the streets, where graffiti protesting about rents were filmed alongside posters, advertisements and mass demonstrations. Compared with the crisply edited techniques deployed in a hard-hitting television documentary, Atkinson's approach seemed lacking in immediate, visceral impact. On a formal level, his organisation of purged and rectilinear elements owed much to Malevich and Mondrian at their most austere. But after a while, his dogged insistence on piling up the evidence paid dividends. The very lack of showmanship or 'artistic' pyrotechnics ensured that nothing distracted attention from the exhibition's central thrust.

Because everyone knows about the social inequalities he exposed at the ICA, they often prove easy to ignore. But Atkinson did not let the visitor evade them for an instant. They were foregrounded at every turn, and viewers also found

Conrad Atkinson, from 'Work, Wages and Prices', 1974.

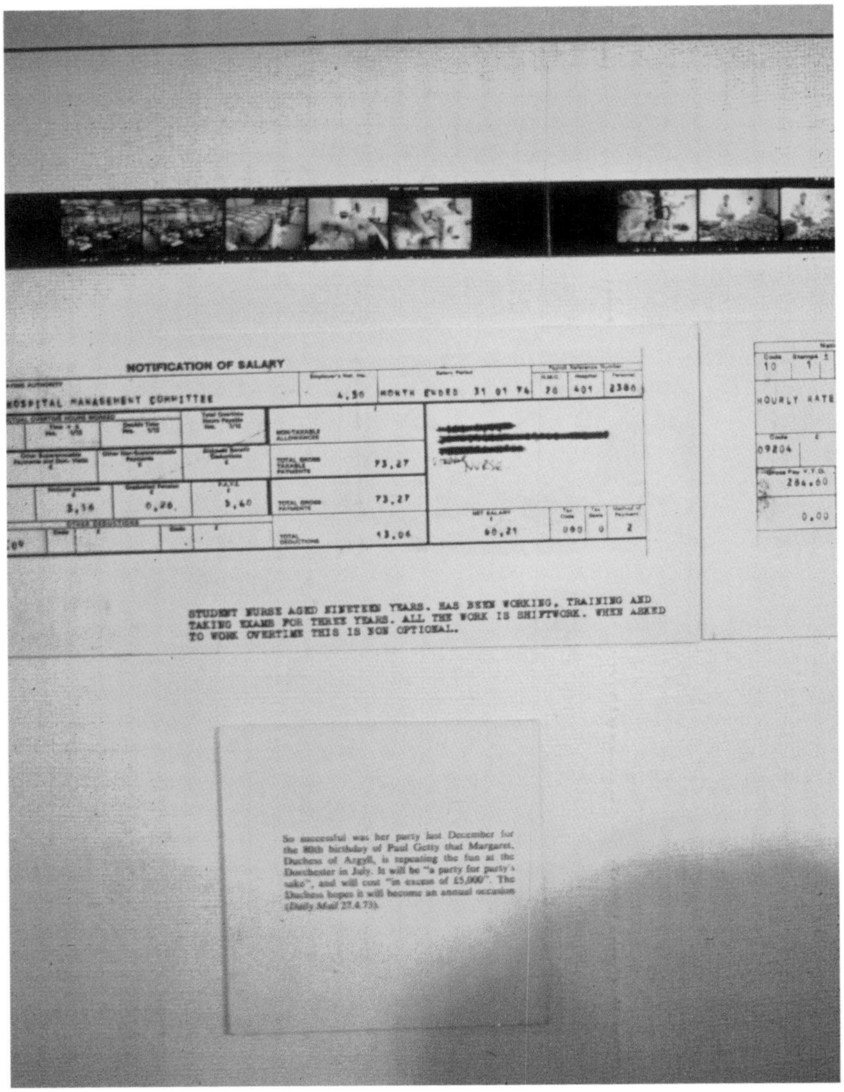

themselves encouraged to participate by supplying comments or contributions of their own. To that extent, Atkinson demonstrated how well he understood the conventions of an art exhibition, establishing a forum for debate throughout the duration of his tough, single-minded show.

A year later, the Arts Council of Northern Ireland and the Irish Congress of Trade Unions asked Atkinson to stage an exhibition in Belfast. While expecting him to tackle an Irish subject, they did not specify what his theme should be. But so far as he was concerned, the chronic political unrest in the country could not be avoided. Travelling round Armagh, Belfast and Derry, Atkinson found that the tragedy of a divided country impinged on his consciousness, and his conscience, wherever he looked. Talking to people, taking photographs, writing notes and collecting found objects, he assembled a profoundly unsettling abundance of material for his exhibition at the Arts Council Gallery in Belfast.

Subsequently shown at Art Net in London, the show was called *A Shade of Green, An Orange Edge*. But if anybody imagined that Atkinson would offer a quiet, pleasing meditation on colour, they were swiftly disillusioned. From the start, he set out to explore the aggression, bitterness, despair and occasional sardonic humour abounding in Northern Irish life. 'No Surrender' cried the slogan painted on a Spar Foodmarket roof. Atkinson's photograph of this resolute graffito set the tone for the rest of the exhibition, riddled as it was with militant defiance on every side. 'This we will maintain' declared the inscription above the Queen's image on a drum, whereas a sticker on a plastic bucket called for 'Troops Out Now.' The heat generated by all these conflicting exhortations was so intense that it did not need any further rhetoric on Atkinson's part. Quite the reverse: the cool, methodical reticence of his marshalling skills threw all the uncompromising hatred into bleak relief. The exhibition gained enormously from the artist's refusal to organise his findings in an emotive way.

Only once did he permit himself to highlight an image with conspicuous drama. Having obtained permission to photograph a bloodsmeared banner that once covered victims of the Bloody Sunday massacre, Atkinson repeated the picture thirteen times in a row. He also included newspaper images of people killed on that terrible day, along with verbal testimonies by eye-witnesses. Written statements played a powerful role in this exhibition, and Atkinson heightened their significance by printing them on green, orange or white cards. Far from using colour in an abstract manner, like so many modernist painters, he let it pinpoint the political sympathies of the statements.

As in *Strike*, Atkinson showed no hesitation in assailing visitors with a daunting profusion of material. But the sheer quantity of visual and verbal information seemed an appropriate way to deal with the avalanche of militant signs and symbols confronting everyone who visits Northern Ireland. Atkinson imprisoned his visitors inside a room packed with explosive comments and equally incendiary images, like the implacable silhouette of a gun daubed on a concrete motorway wall. And he reinforced them with a fusillade of remarks written by people who had reacted strongly to his Belfast instalment of the show. 'God Save Ireland! (Nobody else will)' conveyed a sense of desperation echoed by many, and yet one visitor contributed a note of complaint: 'There are beautiful people, beautiful buildings, beautiful scenes in this country. Why aren't they here, please?'

The contents of Atkinson's show provided its own implicit reply to that bewildered and indignant question. Faced with the gruelling reality of civil struggle, he could not pretend that it somehow did not exist and concentrate instead on pastoral idylls. Besides, he had written in the exhibition catalogue that the show was 'really pointing to priorities and only when the soil bed of such issues is lain will it be possible for me to plant or paint flowers.' His attitude was entirely understandable. Atkinson aimed at using the exhibition as a catalyst for change, even if Northern Ireland's problems appeared so deep-seated that optimism was difficult to sustain. What possible way forward could there be, at a time when everything seemed mired in hatred, violence and mistrust?

One answer lay in the campaign for a Bill of Rights. Impressed by such an eminently achievable cause, Atkinson made sure that the video section of his show focused on discussions of this key issue by the Northern Ireland Civil Rights Association and the Ulster Citizens Civil Liberties Centre. Their stubborn, resolute hope offered a reassuring and much-needed contrast to many of the comments recorded elsewhere in the show, ranging from 'Northern Ireland has a problem for every solution' to the British soldier who protested that 'we are here to be targets while the politicians mark time.'

The most inspirational contribution to the video sequences came from Fenner Brockway, who had given a speech opening Atkinson's show in Belfast. He insisted on cutting through the miasma of negation and declaring that 'there is an extraordinary unanimity of opinion in Northern Ireland about the need for a Bill of Civil Rights.' So at the centre of all the visual images displayed in the exhibition, where partisan murals depicting King William riding a white horse were juxtaposed with diehard citizens wearing clothes emblazoned with patterns from the Union Jack, a palpable source of progress was identified. On one card, Atkinson had recorded a slogan on a Ballymurphy wall asking: 'Is there a life before death?' But his decision to concentrate on the Bill of Rights suggested that despair was premature, and that contemporary artists could lend their energies to a thoroughgoing exploration of the tragedy.

After taking on such an enormous and multi-faceted subject, Atkinson decided in 1978 to aim at a tightly defined target. He was invited, as a member of the Slade School of Art's teaching staff, to make a print for presentation to the Queen Mother. The gift commemorated the 150th anniversary of University College London, and the mood was supposed to be celebratory. Atkinson, however, had no intention of producing an image replete with blandness and self-congratulation. He realised that the chosen date, in April 1978, also marked the twentieth anniversary of the introduction to Britain of Thalidomide, the drug that ended up damaging the lives of too many babies and their families. So he made his Anniversary Print in the style of a glossy advertisement for Distillers (Biochemicals), the company that began marketing Thalidomide in April 1958.

For two years, it was sold across the counter under the trade name 'Distaval', and Atkinson placed this disastrous product in the foreground of his image. Ranged round it, in a majestic still life, were many of the bottles produced by Distillers in their alcoholic drinks range, including Haig Whisky and Gordon's Gin. They were shown against a backdrop of the City of London, dominated by the dome of St Paul's Cathedral. But the most damning part of the print was positioned below this glowing image, where the story of Thalidomide was spelled out in words and statistics. Following its withdrawal in 1961, and the acquisition of Distillers (Biochemicals) by an American Company, the parents of children who had been blighted by the drug struggled to obtain compensation. Atkinson charted the history of Distillers' reluctant and evasive negotiations with the families, as well as the inadequacy of their eventual offers. At the same time, he specified the colossal profits made by the Company. As a final thrust, he noted that 'pleas to Buckingham Palace to withdraw the Royal Warrant from Distillers

Conrad Atkinson, 'A Children's Story (For Her Majesty)', 1978.

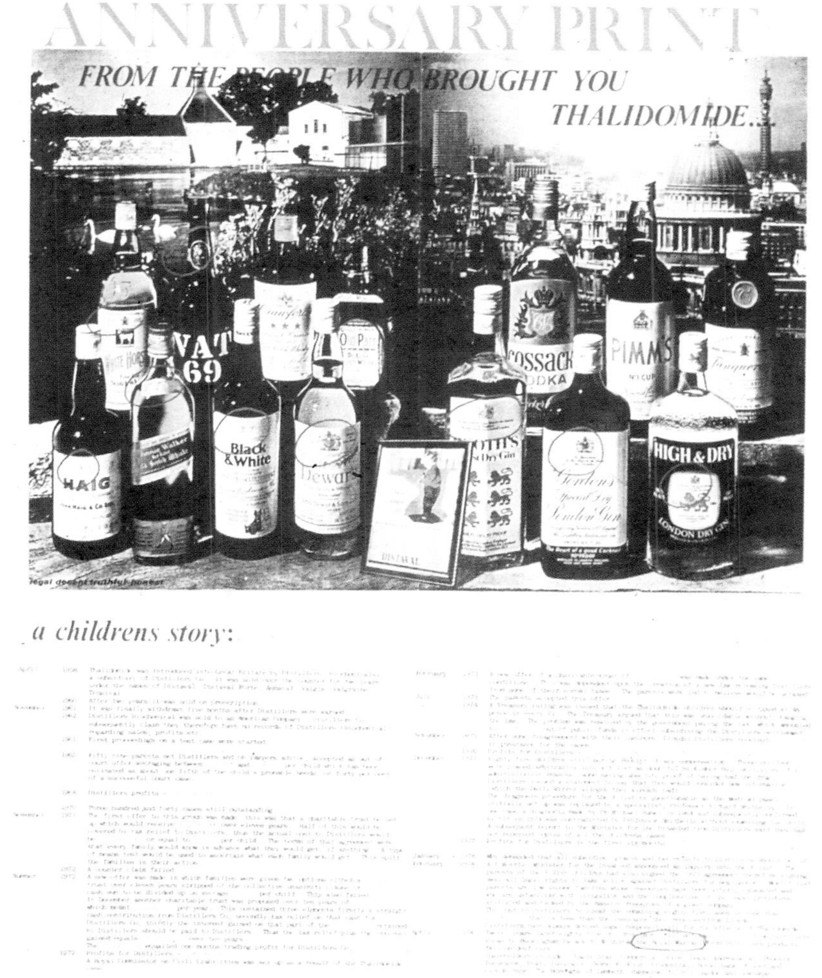

products fell on deaf ears.' Hence his determination to call this print *A Children's Story (For Her Majesty)*. The bottles grouped in the resplendent image were shown with the Royal Warrant ringed on their labels.

As a result, the Queen Mother was left in no doubt about her family's connection to the tragedy, and Atkinson's print became notorious when Derek Boshier purchased a copy for the Arts Council's collection. He then chose it for inclusion in an exhibition called *Lives*. Writing an angry and outspoken text for the catalogue, Atkinson condemned the Royal Family for 'lending its name' to the Distillers Company. He declared that 'the Royal Family and their advisors have shown a deplorable lack of taste and compassion' – a frontal attack that was bound to cause alarm within the highest Arts Council circles. Atkinson was duly summoned to the council headquarters in Piccadilly and told, without any explanation, that his print had been 'withdrawn' from the *Lives* exhibition. Moreover, his accompanying text was removed from the catalogue, following

Conrad Atkinson, detail from 'Sunset: Shelley / Wordsworth', 1978.

'legal advice' taken by the council. After protesting, Atkinson sued the Arts Council for breach of contract and loss of earnings. Two years later, in 1981, he was finally offered compensation and accepted it.

Not that his scrutiny of multinational companies was exhausted. On the contrary: Atkinson's next ICA exhibition, opening in the same year as his settlement with the Arts Council, widened out from Distillers to embrace the overall balance of economic power across the globe. With supreme irony, he couched his show in the language of love. No less than sixteen red hearts were sprayed on the ICA's white walls. They appeared to be the work of a graffiti artist celebrating Valentine's Day, but there was nothing affectionate about the contents of the first heart encountered by exhibition visitors. Inside a watercolour image of a world map, small white cards were assembled in rows with disturbing facts to convey. One of them disclosed that 'in 1979 nearly one third of all world trade was from sales and transfers within Multinational corporations.' Different aspects of this disturbing imbalance were scrutinised by other cards, including South America's subservience to a single megacompany's ultra-assertive ambitions.

But Atkinson did not confine himself solely to dissecting big-business monopolies across the globe. In the second heart, he painted a yellow butterfly whose body and wings were choked with packets and tins of insect killer, vegetable pest duster and bird repellent spray. The user-friendly packaging with its purring texts – 'now in ready measured sachets' – failed to disguise the unsettling, lethal power of these horticultural weapons. Nor did Atkinson become any less uncompromising in the other hearts. The danger of everything from radiation leakage to irresponsible slimming advertisements was highlighted with the aid of newspaper cuttings, postcard views of verdant landscapes and an abundance of other, carefully selected material. By cramming each heart with so much alarming evidence, he also implied that the body of the world had become congested to bursting-point.

Even when the images suggested jauntiness, they turned out to reflect a deplorable global malaise. A dog appeared in the seventh heart, assembled with considerable wit and vivacity from pet food packets. But its frisky, outflung limbs and erect tail were made from the delicacies that wealthy owners lavish on their animals. Whether 'Good Boy Choc Drops' or 'complete moist meals in individual airtight packs – seafood flavour', they testified to the money lavished on these cosseted favourites. And the two fragments of paper kicked by the dog's hind legs describe how underdeveloped countries, plagued by famine and malnutrition, export an abundance of quality protein to the West. It is a pernicious waste of resources, for the majority of this precious protein is consumed by livestock and pets. While African children starve, our four-legged friends are heaped with an embarrassment of culinary delicacies.

Nor did Atkinson's indictment stop there. The hearts painted on the other wall were stricken with a whole array of different afflictions, including South African apartheid, the threat posed by nuclear extinction, the legacy of Vietnam and growth of arms manufacturing. Verbal information was given pictorial vitality by watercolour camouflage designs and other pictorial diversions. But the words carried the most unnerving disclosures, like the admission that 'a recent American Alert signalled world-wide preparing all aircraft for takeoff was a mistake, due to the running of a war-game programme on a military computer without switching out the connection to the Alert system.'

Conscious perhaps that he might risk wearying the ICA's visitors with a surfeit of words, Atkinson provided respite on the gallery's floor. For the hour-glass arranged there was largely reliant on its visual power alone. Time appeared to be running out within the glass, where one half was engorged with a superfluity of food, armaments and media overkill while the other half contained only funereal leaves and empty food-bowls. Here, Atkinson reduced the clamour on the walls to a stark, ruthlessly simplified confrontation between rampant excess and destitution. It was plainly intended to stir the onlooker's conscience, and nothing has happened in the decades since this exhibition to ameliorate the ills he deplored.

Moving incessantly between the particular and the universal, Atkinson has devoted much of his subsequent work to generating an awareness of malevolent aggression on the one hand and acute suffering on the other. The deliberate sobriety of his early work, with its emphasis on marshalled facts and documentary images, gave way to a more oblique and visually seductive approach.

It appeared initially in some work stimulated by Atkinson's revaluation of Shelley and Wordsworth. Searching for an English tradition to which he could re-

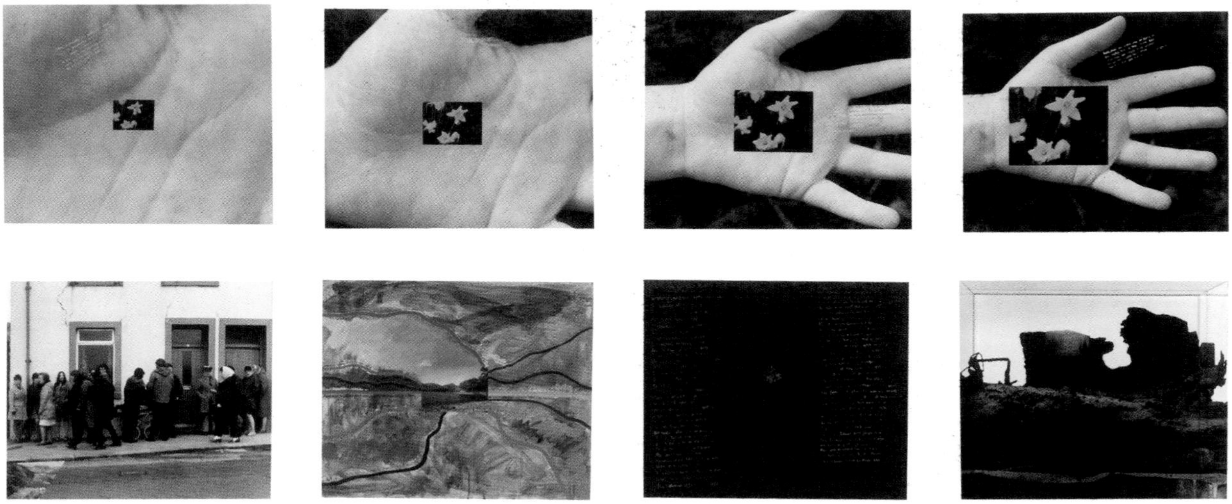

Conrad Atkinson, 'For Wordsworth; For West Cumbria', 1981 (Tate Gallery).

Details overleaf.

late his own work, he found it in Romantic literature. When studying Wordsworth at school, Atkinson had impatiently concluded that the Laureate of the Lakes had no relevance for the people he grew up with on the coastal industrial strip. Subsequently, however, he realised that the young Wordsworth had been fired by an intense revolutionary fervour. Re-reading 'The Ruined Cottage', Atkinson admired Wordsworth's readiness to write about the dilemma of a couple forced to leave their home and, while it decayed, find work elsewhere. The area where Atkinson spent his childhood was similarly blighted, especially in comparison with the contemporary Lake District where tourism thrived and holiday or 'second' homes abounded. So he devoted a major, sixteen-foot work to a meditation called *For Wordsworth; For West Cumbria*, and its acquisition by the Tate Gallery in 1981 meant that his work was now encountered by a wider audience than before. It also ushered in a desire on his part to replace what he called 'bunches of statistics' with a new emphasis on the personal within the collective.

When Atkinson had explored iron-ore mining, he studied hands clubbed and swollen by pneumoconiosis. It inaugurated his fascination with the metaphor of the human body, and *For Wordsworth; For West Cumbria* is dominated in the top row by the motif of the outstretched hand. At first the palm is enormous, containing at its centre a diminutive image of nature. But by the end, the hand has shrunk to a minuscule size in relation to the vastly enlarged nature behind. Quotations from Wordsworth, including a heartfelt passage describing how his brother's death at sea transformed the poet's attitude to nature, accompany these images. And then, on the bottom row, Atkinson's own angry images of industrial West Cumbria offer a stark alternative. The Brannan's strike picket is followed by the plight of a nineteenth-century iron-ore miner, whose life was ruined by dispossession. Leaping between past and present, Atkinson encompasses in succeeding panels the death of West Cumbrian migrants on a North Sea oil rig, and a worker at Windscale nuclear power station killed by leukemia at the age of 36. The whole complex work terminates in a bleak image of the unemployment office at Cleator Moor, ironically juxtaposed with a montaged reference to the

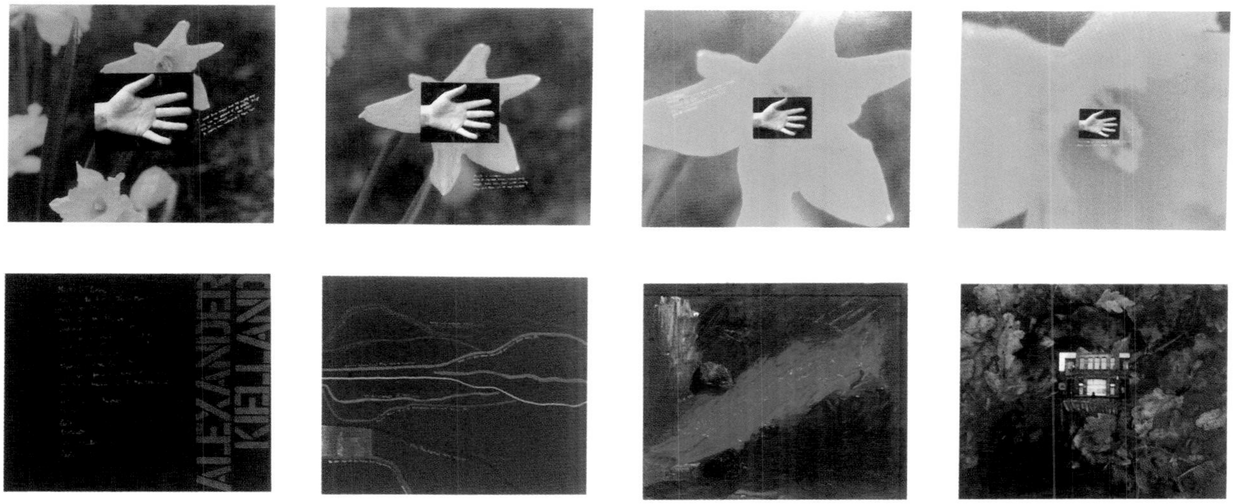

Lake District. Taken in its entirety, *For Wordsworth; For West Cumbria* takes an impassioned stand against smug, unquestioning ideas about the English landscape. And it is informed by personal anguish, for Atkinson suspects that his own mother and father both died from their working involvement with Windscale.

At heart, the tragedy of human suffering underpins all the disparate subjects Atkinson has tackled. Just as he revivified our understanding of Wordsworth by placing his poetry in the context of Cumbrian unemployment and death, so he prompted us to look with fresh eyes at the Courtauld Collection's medieval and Renaissance paintings. During his period there as Distinguished Visiting Professor in 2002, he became preoccupied with images of matryrdom. Focusing on the idea of 'beautiful mutilations', he realised that the bloodiest and most tortured Courtauld paintings related to his involvement with the imagery of modem war. He aimed at 'breaking open the collection, like a wound', and visitors found Atkinson's work dramatically intervening in the normal gallery display.

'Aesthetics can be a pretty ugly business' announced a digitised embroidery inscription on a Daniel Hechter wool suit. As if to bear out the truth of this paradoxical assertion, Atkinson extracted the gash in Christ's side from a Fra Angelico predella panel. Transferred to a jacket, the blood-soaked wound made the garment resemble evidence discovered at the location of a murder. He even removed the leaves covering Adam and Eve's genitals in a Cranach painting. They were turned into vine-leaf motifs ornamenting the base of a glazed and gold-lustre ceramic. But any suspicion that Atkinson had turned the leaves into decorative devices was allayed by our realisation that the seductive, glinting ceramic took the form of a land-mine.

Heavily involved with land-mine campaigns over the last decade, Atkinson returns now to the Lake District even more determined to reveal the most radical strain in Wordsworth's vision of the landscape. Before the Romantic era, travellers passing through the Lakes often shunned the terrain. But in his finest poetry, Wordsworth conveyed the full complexity of his clear-eyed response to his homeland, and he was even prepared to arrive at the desolate admission that 'the

industrial hazards pneumoconiosis cancer
Alienated picturesque
socially constructed landscape

To make those small farms into one
Others must quit as well as you
All our remonstrances did fail,
So of our goods we made a sale,
And, with many a heartfelt tear,
We left the home we loved so dear;
That we a livelihood might gain.
'Twould be in vain for me to show
The hardships we'd to undergo,
The full amount of our distress.
My parents succumbed to the blow;
Death soon did ease them of their woe;
We from each other then were squandered,
Two brothers and two sisters dear
Did o'er the broad Atlantic steer,
And found a home and are at rest,
In the wild prairies of the West;
One brother still in Ireland, and one
Has to Australian gold fields gone,
And I, oppressed and troubled sore,
resolved to quit my native,
And into England take a tour,
So here I am on Clinton Moor.
Dick Watson an Iron Ore Miner 1888

things which I have seen I now can see no more.' Atkinson persuades us to look at Wordsworth's vision of nature all over again. And *Common Sights*, his exhibition at the Wordsworth Trust, is not afraid to deal with even the most sacrosanct material in audacious new ways.

Atkinson is at his boldest in the textual pieces, where he has the temerity to allow some of Wordsworth's most celebrated poems to be invaded by provocative song writers and rappers of today. Kurt Cobain's suicidal meditation on emotional numbness and heroin abuse is permitted to penetrate Wordsworth's 'To a Butterfly'. But nothing is more calculated to unsettle traditional devotees of the Laureate than Atkinson's radical version of 'Ode: Intimations of Immortality'. Eminem's unbridled rap greeting, 'Hi there little boys and girls (FUCK YOU!)' is allowed to kick-start Atkinson's alternative version. Only then does he allow Wordsworth's sorrowful first line, 'There was a time when meadow, grove, and stream', to enter the poem. From then on, Eminem and Wordsworth fight it out, line after conflicting line. The urge to 'poison squirrels' clashes with 'the earth and every common sight', while 'celestial light' comes up against retarded Bob who 'sits at home and smokes pot.' Gradually, this bizarre interpolation strategy begins to pay off. By the time Wordsworth arrives at the elegiac admission that his childhood vision of nature has been lost, his despair is envenomed by Eminem's everdarkening story of Bob lurking in the nocturnal parking lot for waitresses he wants to murder.

The most powerful part of the poem intercuts between his killings in the woods and Wordsworth's yearning references to the moon's 'delight' or 'waters on a starry night.' They become unexpectedly sinister, and Eminem monopolises the final lines now that the overall mood has grown so rancid. Terminating in a cri de coeur about a penis 'the size of a peanut', coupled with warnings about the lethal effect of ecstasy, Atkinson's heretical work nevertheless gives new life to the despair in Wordsworth's grim insistence that 'there hath past away a glory from the earth.' With a shock, we realise how this venerated line could have a bearing on our contemporary afflictions as well, including the corrosive evils that Atkinson has spent his career as an artist striving to pinpoint, expose and, in the end, arraign.

Common Sights

CONRAD ATKINSON

The aspects underpinning my interest in Wordsworth and his work could be simply described as being focused upon the material world and the intellectual sphere and their concurrent relationship. The former is an apparently solid unyielding physical presence and the second less discernible with gray areas containing multiple notions including aesthetics and emotion, sensibility and subjectivity. Looking at these aspects of our existence and examining these twin concepts the phrase 'All that's solid melts into air' seems to contain enough truth that the slopes of the mountains and valleys of certainty and meaning are filled with so many attitudes and possibilities that we could be forgiven for freezing ourselves with a fear of acting or thinking about our environment and its meaning. Possibilities that have arisen in recent years might well be described as corporate and commercialized ways of seeing our surroundings and our landscapes which are so ubiquitous as to obliterate our presences and fill our visions with dubious other agendas. Constantly contesting these meanings could paralyze our desire and our will as well as our ability to act or even think 'cause every time I write a rhyme, these people think it's a crime'.

These concepts skate and slide and dance and reel; they flit and trip and slither and seep and trickle and crawl; they flow and stroll and run and wriggle and are tossed through our landscapes.

The temporary landscape flickers in and out of our vision and our mind because there was a time when every common sight did seem fixed and ok but then they change and every body loses itself.

Some strange landscapes both material and intellectual exist in the realm of landmines, with which I've worked for a decade. Working with landmines experts in Mines Advisory Group (MAG)) and with the US Campaign to Ban Landmines (Vietnam Veterans Trust) I was vividly made aware of this notion of the intangible interior reflecting the exterior landscape. A landmines removal expert came back from Cambodia recently and at one of my exhibitions said to me that when he returned to England he found it difficult to walk on an English lawn. Possibly the most famous example of this mental shift is the story of Gray drawing the curtains of his carriage as he drove through the Lake District in order not to view the brutal mountains. Wordsworth removed the curtains in a blinding flash. Subsequently after the death of his brother John at sea Wordsworth writes that he is no longer able to look at the sea … 'the things I once could see I now can see no more'.

The notion that aboriginal people in Australia relate deeply to the landscape poetically and through stories and drawings and dreamings and coloring their bodies with red and yellow ochre they turn themselves into their landscapes as the distinctions and separations between their bodies and their minds and their landscapes slips away like a mirage … my own experience as a child in Cleator Moor of

the 'redmen', the iron ore miners, the red iron ore dust seeping and transforming their clothes into glittering fine silk like postmodern *haute couture* as they walked home with lungs of dust through a landscape permeated with red. The dust is now mined as a colorant for makeup. This landscape is colored by the vast hidden body of iron ore under the town; making the streams red, the town overlooked by two great slag banks studded with pumice reeked with familiar sulphur, garden rockeries made with spa, paths lined with crystals from the mines, crushed red gravel on the footpaths through the town, doorstops of polished hematite beside the reddened doorsteps, the red offcuts of pit props carried underarm at the end of the shift for the fire at home … St Mary's Catholic Church with the Grotto of life sized saints embedded in iron ore spoil from the pits and built by the unemployed miners who made quartz boxes in a hall in Cleator Moor called The Blood Tub … all overlooked by two huge slag banks studded with pumice, and slag with sulphur seeping through the white and gray ash. These sulphurous fumes enabling the miners to grow beautiful disease free roses. An almost contrived fairytale paradox of beauty thriving in a poisonous atmosphere. The landscape from under the ground … the world turned upside down. I watched a couple of miners deep underground amongst glittering hematite fragments working with small pickaxes delicately and skillfully loosening a giant body of ore from the wall; they took over three hours sensing each transient vibration through the earth listening watching speaking.

This sense of landscape dissolving the body is reflected in other artists like Emily Bronte's *Wuthering Heights* where the characters names are taken from the landscape; Heathcliff, Hareton, Nellie Dean, Lockwood, Thrushcross Grange … people and the environment streaming through each other. The body and the mind the material and the emotional smearing themselves with each other's colors.

Pamela Woof talks about this in her essay on Daffodils:

> How personal, even modern is Dorothy's reaction to the daffodils … Her perception of the flowers frail and mortal as we know they are, is original … no moral is drawn; it simply was so … this is deliberate writing

Dorothy's precise observation of the daffodils moving as human bodies is resonant and unsentimental.

The way Wordsworth explores the emotional and intellectual and our landscapes relationships with the material world is both subtle and startlingly direct. There is astonishing clarity in his question to the old leech gatherer, a transient worker in the poem 'Resolution and Independence': 'How is it that you live, and what is it you do?'

The inquiry has no element of condescension and it is addressed to everyone and everything in the universe. It is perhaps the single most important question in literature after 'To be or not to be, that is the question'.

A greeting in Cleator Moor I remember from the forties and fifties was "Are you working?"

Lyrical Ballads discovered the internal and external in a direct, radical and familiar language. Common stories about and about us. As the industrial revolution was turning whitehot from Whitehaven to Manchester and the migration to the cities increasingly put a gold frame turning the landscape into the picturesque. George Morland's rural poor disappear from Constable's landscapes.

We know the landscape is manipulated materially and physically, but more complex and less focussed upon is how the landscape is managed internally, how is it manipulated aesthetically, emotionally, poetically, politically, ideologically; we know the production and marketing reasons which construct political apples and economic steaks but who constructs its meanings and for what purpose? How is the manipulation of the landscapes of our desires and emotions created and by what poetic, aesthetic and politics does it operate? How would the divinely and infinitely curious guy called Wordsworth have responded to the invisibility of the poetic residues of power? About the half life of things, the low thresholds, and americium, and strontium 90 and distorted insects and plutonium and seasonal labor patterns of the tourist industry and agribusiness and dioxin and 245t and genetically modified crops and global warming, West Nile disease and foot and mouth and the approaching blue tongue disease and BSE … and Africa moving slowly north in hunger. This is the man who democratized the landscape and the language with which it was constructed … paradoxically in his 'other' life as a sort of Tory he was famously hostile to democratic access to the land in his opposition to opening up the Lake District to the masses … but in essence his real life was elsewhere.

Robert Woof points out that 'a new question today is that cross pollination between the wild daffodil and the cultivar will lead to the destruction of the daffodils the Wordsworths celebrated. Left to the rigors of nature, it seems that the cultivars tend to revert to 'blind' plants, producing few if any flowers eventually.'

These common unseen sights are smothered or erased in gold and obliterated by corporate pictures. How can we mean? How can we see? How can we react? How can we speak? How can we mean? How can we feel? How can we desire? Whose desires, whose images, whose fantasy, whose life, whose meanings, for who's benefit, whose landscapes, whose pictures? Who is approaching to the nature of the ocular spectrum and every common sight? With no more wild daffodils.

'I've used the pen to express myself. You'll see that from day one my main focus was on self expression, no matter how lewd the subject matter.' This is Eminem talking recently about his work and acknowledging an acute awareness of the notion of lewdness and of the objections to his subject matter (as opposed to his language which is in itself innovative).

Compare this with the scorn directed at Wordsworth's subject matter, daffodils, in a letter by the poet Anna Seward to Walter Scott:

> Surely if his worst foe had chosen to caricature this egoistic manufacturer of metaphysic importance upon trivial themes, he could not have done it more effectively.

My early work (I make no mention of quality comparisons with myself and the two artists quoted) was attacked viciously for its subject matter … the lives of common people and their diseases … asbestosis, mercury poisoning, emphysema, pneumoconiosis the landscapes and their bodies.

> The mind of man is married to this goodly universe

Conrad Atkinson, 'William Wordsworth I', 2003.

Conrad Atkinson, 'William Wordsworth II', 2003.

Conrad Atkinson, 'William Wordsworth III', 2003.

Conrad Atkinson, 'William Wordsworth IV', 2003.

Conrad Atkinson, 'Dancing', 2003.

Conrad Atkinson, 'Golden', 2003.

Conrad Atkinson, 'Collaboration: Eminem, Wordsworth, Atkinson', 2003.

Conrad Atkinson, 'Working together: Bill, Kurt and Conrad', 2003.

Suit

The suit made in Savile Row which Wordsworth wore on Thursday 15th April 1802 whilst walking home from Eusemere to Grasmere with his sister Dorothy in a furious wind. It was on this walk that they observed many flowers and then fairly suddenly a large number of daffodils. A couple of years after this walk Wordsworth wore the suit to write the poem Daffodils and a little later he gave the suit to Coleridge to wear as a lucky literary suit in which to write popular poetry. Coleridge immediately wrote Kubla Khan which was an instant hit. The suit disappeared one night from a public house in Keswick in 1816 and was recently found in a thrift shop in San Francisco by Conrad Atkinson. Atkinson a minor Cumbrian artist living in San Francisco subsequently researched its provenance during lunch at Zuni Restaurant on Market Street (one of the best in San Francisco for Classic Californian cuisine) whilst eating a Caesar salad accompanied by a glass of chilled Hess Select Chardonnay.

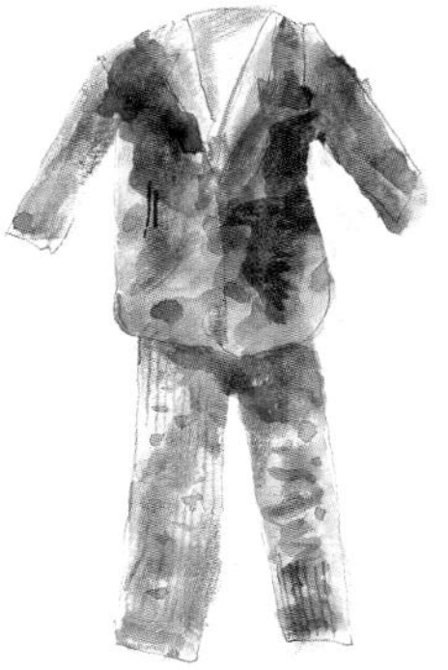

The suit contained pollen from the English native wild daffodil Narcissus pseudo-narcissus. L. It might be pointed out that this daffodil is under threat from the many hybrids produced in recent years by genetic modification.

The pollen grain was identified by its morphology, which is ellipsoidal with a single long slit like aperture. Beneath the proteins and lipids on the surface of the pollen is a reticulum resembling lacelike vermicelli. The pollen grains are between 50 and 60 microns long. This pollen was then dated to about 1802 with an accuracy of plus or minus four years; it was then subjected to further tests which located the specific area by the lake mentioned in Dorothy's diary. An analysis of the ink stains on the suit were found to contain iron (possibly from Cleator Moor iron ore mine which was located just behind Atkinsons birthplace on Birks Road) which matched the extremely rare ink used by Coleridge in the original draft of the Kubla Khan.

Conrad Atkinson, September 2003

Flat Roofs

HENRY SHUKMAN

A tennis ball grown shaggy;
a packet of ten crumbling into pulp;
a dented Heineken can still in its four-pack collar.
It hasn't rained for days
but there are vestigial puddles here
brightening the asphalt with a grating of sky.
Two banks of windows
give into gloomy underwater offices:
anglepoises like corals, forgotten wastes of blotter,
of sandy desk and battlegrey fishglued carpet-tile.
And this their view: this little tank
of daylight with its hoard of neglect.
We used to seek places such as this.
We'd park our bikes, climb by ledge and pipe,
get our knees onto the parapet,
and beachcomb for old balls, for packs
that might have one overlooked last
nestled in their still-bright foil.
Especially on Sundays, days that were themselves
the abandoned and deserted of the week.
It was here we began to build our lives,
in the first spaces we knew
unclaimed and free.

Henry Shukman is a writer in residence at the Wordsworth Trust. This poem was written as a contribution to the exhibition 'Common Sights' by Conrad Atkinson.

Conrad Atkinson

Chronology, selected major group and solo exhibitions

1940	Born in Cleator Moor, Cumbria, England
1957–61	Carlisle College of Art
1961–62	Liverpool College of Art
1962–65	Royal Academy, awarded David Murray Scholarship
1965	Abby Minor Travelling Scholarship
1970–80	Exhibits in the UK and Ireland, including:
1970	Sigi Krauss Gallery, London, *Garbage Strike* with the Fluxus group
1972	First solo exhibition at the Institute of Contemporary Art, London, *Strike*; Tooth's Gallery, London, *Critic's Choice*
1974	ICA and Northern Arts Gallery, Newcastle, *Work, Wages and Prices*
1975	Arts Council of Northern Ireland Gallery, Belfast, *A Shade of Green, an Orange Edge*; *Five Banners* work for the General and Municipal Workers Union carried on several marches during this year
1976	Art Net, Nottingham, *Northern Ireland 1968, Mayday*
1979–80	Carlisle Museum and Art Gallery and tour, *Conrad Atkinson: Selected Works About The North*
1979–85	Begins to exhibit in the USA, Canada and Australia
1979	Ronald Feldman Fine Arts, New York, *Material*
1982	Ronald Feldman Fine Arts, New York, *Separate Pieces*
1985	Artist in residence, Lewisham
1985	Ronald Feldman Fine Arts, New York, *Goldfish*
1987	London Underground posterworks and billboards, commissioned by Art Angel, Newcastle and Project UK
1987	Artist in residence, Edinburgh University
1988	Cleator Moor, *The Miner's Monument*: commission by Cleator Moor Town Council

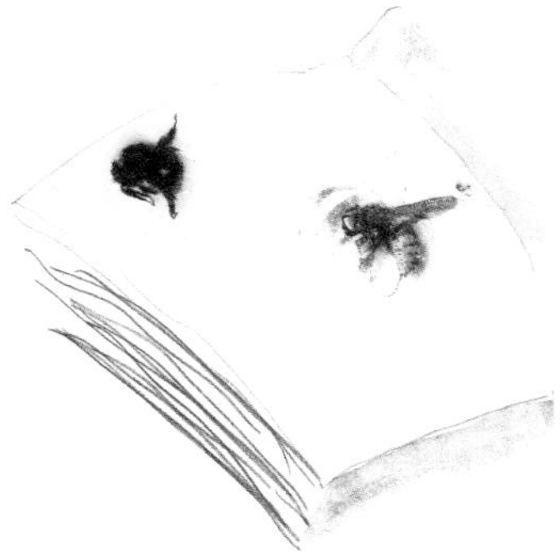

1989	Victoria & Albert Museum, London, *Newspaper Works*; Ronald Feldman Fine Arts, New York, *Front Pages*
1992	Becomes Professor of Art, University of California at Davis, USA
1993	Henry Moore Sculpture Trust Studio, *For Emily*
1993	Moscow ICA, *Newsflies*
1995	University Art Gallery and Museum, Berkeley, *Dorothy, Diego, Theodore and a Horse of a Different Color*
1996	Tullie House, Carlisle, *Transient*
1997	West Cumbria College, *Mining Culture*
1997	Appointed official artist of the US Campaign to ban land mines (Vietnam Veterans Trust)
1998	Artist in residence, Kecskemet, Hungary
2000	Abbott Hall Art Gallery, Kendal, *Ethical Viruses: Twenty Years*
2000	Artist in residence, Villeroy and Boch, Gustausburg, Sweden
2002	Courtauld Gallery, London, *Excavated Mutilations*; Wolverhampton City Art Gallery, *Strike*
2003	White Box, New York, *Constantly Contesting*; Ronald Feldman Fine Arts, New York, *Installation*; The Wordsworth Trust, Grasmere, *Common Sights*

Notes on contributors

RICHARD CORK is an art critic, historian, broadcaster and exhibition organiser. For many years a writer for the *Evening Standard*, he is now senior art critic at *The Times*; his most recent publication is a four-volume collection of his critical writings since the 1970s, published this year by Yale University Press.

HENRY SHUKMAN is a writer in residence at the Wordsworth Trust. He has twice been shortlisted for the Forward Prize, and his first collection of verse, *In Dr. No's Garden* (Cape, 2002) won the Aldeburgh Festival prize; a first novel, *Darien Dogs*, will be published next year.

ROBERT WOOF has been the Director of the Wordsworth Trust since 1989. His most recent book is *William Wordsworth: The Critical Heritage 1793–1820*, published by Routledge in 2001.